A
Alph[...]
of
Alluring
Words

by

Gawain Armstrong

With illustrations by
Chloe Rodham

ERGO
PRESS
Publishing for Northumberland

AN ALPHABET OF ALLURING WORDS

Published by
ERGO PRESS
© Gawain Armstrong 2006
Illustrated by Chloe Rodham

ISBN: 0-9552758-4-9
ISBN: 978-0-9552758-4-5

Printed by Robson Print Ltd, Hexham
using 100% recycled paper

ERGO
PRESS
5, St Mary's Chare
Hexham
Northumberland
NE46 1NQ

ergo.press@yahoo.co.uk
www.ergopress.com

Written, illustrated, published and printed in Northumberland

Cover graphics by Harriet McDougall

*I*ntroduction

This is a book of twenty six words chosen for their interest and for their beauty of sound and of meaning alike. W. B. Yeats said, "Think like a wise man but communicate in the language of the people". I'm not sure that I agree with him; at the very least it must surely depend upon which 'people' he's talking about. The ubiquity of rapid communication by text message and e-mail means that the 'people' are unlikely to use a large proportion of the many thousands of words available – it is too time consuming to search for the *mot juste* – even supposing a vocabulary wide enough to hold it.

This is a subjective selection of favourite words; some I use regularly, others rarely. All are useful and – when used correctly – say exactly what they mean to say. I have given an example of how each may be used, but some readers may disagree with my interpretation, which is all part of the pleasure of using alluring words. If enough people send me better examples, or other compelling words, I will write another book.

Gawain Armstrong
July 2006

The difference between the almost right word and
the right word is really a large matter –
'tis the difference between the lightning bug
and the lightning.

Mark Twain

Anomie

Emile Durkheim was the first to define the concept of *anomie* in his book *Suicide* of 1897. As used today, anomie describes a state of mind and being in which norms of behaviour and values are ignored or (worse still) unknown. It is, for example, *anomie* that afflicts the young people who engage in the pastime of 'happy-slapping', an oxymoron if ever there were one.

*B*acchanalian

If you've been out for an evening of carousing, drunken merrymaking, then Bacchanalian is the word you need to describe it. Originally, the Bacchanalia were fairly wild, mystical festivals to the Roman God, Bacchus, also known as Dionysus. These were of particular notoriety because at first only *women* were allowed to attend, and because cult members included slaves and the poor; for these and other reasons the Bacchanalia were prohibited from 186BC. Used today, the word refers to any boisterous revelry of an inebriated kind, usually with a certain amount of disorder.

*C*asuistry

This is an important word that has rather fallen into disrepute. Casuistic reasoning is part of English common law, being the method used in case-based reasoning; in contrast to a Kantian, legalistic method of deciding a legal or moral issue, casuistry is essentially utilitarian. Kant would say that lying is always wrong, the casuist might argue that experience shows us that sometimes lying can save lives. Using casuistry, past examples of legal findings are analysed and conclusions are drawn, which are then applied to a particular ethical question or legal case.

The problem with casuistry lies not so much with its principle as with its use. As a pejorative term it implies the use of subtle – even specious – reasoning to win an argument; in this sense of the word, the use of casuistry is intended to mislead an adversary. Thus, one who uses a clever, slippery argument to achieve his end is often accused of casuistry.

Deism

Many people today are deists, (from the Latin for God) rather than theists (from the Greek for God), which is why it's important to know the difference. As a result of Enlightenment thinking, many religious believers came to reject the idea of a God known through revelation – a God who reveals himself through prophets, miracles etc. However, they held on to a belief in God based on human reason, experience and nature.

Deists will infer the existence of God from the complex and orderly nature of the universe; they may even *feel* God with their senses. What they will *not* do is believe that Scripture is God's Word, nor that organised religion is other than man made. They would say that we can use our reason to ponder about what God *may* be, but that as humans we have no words to define God, no means of understanding him.

Egregious

There are lots of words for something or somebody who is conspicuously offensive, but this is my favourite. Smarmy salesmen, 1960s architecture, illiterate advertising copy and junk food are all outstandingly awful and therefore egregious. It is the only word properly to describe the outrageous Mr Collins in Jane Austen's *Pride and Prejudice*.

*F*op

A fop is a dandy, a beau – one who is vain and affected both in manner and dress. Unlike the *fops* of the past, today's 'neo-fops' are not generally men of leisure like George (*Beau*) Brummel of the Regency period, who took five hours to dress and who recommended that boots be polished with champagne. It costs money to be *genuinely* foppish, and the obvious modern exemplars are footballers – who would have thought it!

G*auleiter*

Everyone has come across a latter day *gauleiter* at some time or another. The term was originally used for chief officials of districts in Germany under the Nazi régime, but in modern usage it applies to any petty official who wields his authority in a pompous, heavy handed fashion. An obvious example would be the traffic warden who continues to put a ticket on a windscreen even as the driver arrives to remove his car …

*H*ubris

Hubris is overweening arrogance – the sort that simply invites retribution or disaster! Those of us who have taken the trouble to understand Islam, and in particular to grasp the essential differences between Sunni and Shi'a, know that without a doubt it is hubris on the part of President Bush to believe that America can impose the American brand of democratic order on Iraq. To announce, as he did when Saddam Hussein was captured, that "all Iraqis can now *come together* and reject violence and build a new Iraq" was an example of pure, purblind hubris.

I ncipient

Something that's incipient is in its initial stages or is about to come into existence. A synonym might be *inchoate*, another alluring word. The thickening waist of the young man with a pint in his hand is an incipient beer belly. The toddler who goes unchecked as he deliberately hurts other children may well be an incipient bully. A meeting held by a shop steward could be an incipient strike ... This is a good term because it can be used in place of several other less interesting words.

*J*ejune

Jejune is a most useful adjective to describe dull, lifeless things. I first heard it used in relation to today's 'enervated Anglican worship' as compared to that experienced in charismatic churches, to which (apparently) the Holy Spirit brings vitality and oomph. Originally meaning 'lacking in nutritive value', it can be used quite widely to describe anything that is dry or insipid. Health and Safety leaflets, prison food and most parliamentary debates are jejune.

_K_ismet

Kismet is an exotic synonym for _fate,_ or _destiny._ The word is Turkish but comes originally from the Persian for _lot._ It can have the implication of _God's will_ for the Muslim, since it also means _predestination._ Apart from the one God, there are also three witches or goddesses, daughters of Zeus and Themis, associated by Greek tradition with human fate:

> _"These are Clotho, Lachesis and Atropos_
> _And they give mortals their share of good and evil"_

(Hesiod, Theogony: 905-6)

So, kismet can be blamed – or thanked – for just about anything!

*L*achrymose

This must be used rather sparingly, and *not* preceded by 'waxed'. It means tearful, weeping or having a tendency to weep. It can also (slightly differently) mean morose or lugubrious, but these are not synonyms: Eeyore is morose, but he isn't lachrymose. In Alice in Wonderland, the Mock Turtle is lachrymose, as are many of the female characters in the novels of Charles Dickens. It should only be used when the subject is showing or feeling *sincere* sorrow – otherwise it sounds affected and unnecessary.

Meretricious

I love this word, not least because many people think that it means the opposite of what it actually does (being confused with *merit worthy*) hence its inclusion in this book. Although it is originally and correctly used when discussing prostitution – for example, a couple may have a *meretricious relationship* – this is not the meaning I have in mind; it is also, beguilingly, used to refer to something that is falsely attractive or tawdry. A meretricious argument is plausible but insincere. Mawkish sentimentality is meretricious; Modern Art may be, as is much of the advertising with which we are bludgeoned.

$\mathcal{N}$ous

Pronounced to rhyme with mouse, this is a particularly useful word. It comes from the Greek where it's pronounced *noose,* meaning 'intellect' or 'mind'. In print it's often put in italics to indicate that it's a foreign import. In modern usage it encompasses common sense as well, which is why it is so handy. Someone with *nous* is clever *and* practical. Learnéd people know things, wise people understand things, efficient people can do things – but employers need people with *nous*. It's a good word to find in a reference.

O*psimath*

An opsimath is an old dog that wants to be taught new tricks. In the past, retirement heralded the onset of old age, the beginning of the end of life's progress. Now we have the University (though it isn't one) of the Third Age, *U3A*, for those who have left full time work and who wish to pursue educational interests with others of a similar age, some well into their nineties, opsimaths all. It's never too late to learn.

$\mathcal{P}$langent

I have included this word as much for its texture and sound as for its meaning. Plangent is another word for orotund or resonant – the song of the whale, the bells of the great Russian cathedrals, the singing of Kathleen Ferrier – all are plangent. It can also have the implication of mournfulness: listen to the sound as the choir reaches the climax of John Tavener's *Song for Athene* …. "Weeping at the grave creates the song: Alleluia". Profound and plangent.

Querulous

It is interesting to note that most of the synonyms for querulous are themselves rather alluring: it means peevish, whining or fretful …all interesting words. It comes straight from the Latin for 'to complain' – but not all complaining is *petulant*, and there is definitely something of that nature about one who is querulous. Jane Austen's tiresome Mrs Bennet provides a good illustration. Sad to say, many of us grow querulous with age. At the stage before we are completely *sans teeth, sans eyes, sans taste, sans everything,* we grow waspish as our powers fail.

Recondite

When something is difficult to penetrate, like the poetry of T S Eliot, it is recondite. Is the literature you are reading full of hidden meaning? Is the lecture to which you are listening incomprehensible to one with ordinary understanding? Recondite is the word you need to define anything so abstruse. It actually comes from the Latin for 'to put away', so that it can be used for something hard to understand or for something of which obscure knowledge is necessary, such as semiotics. This is not a pejorative term; something recondite is generally deep but worth the effort to understand it.

*S*obriquet

A sobriquet is a nickname. Why use this word? Because sometimes nickname is too clipped and familiar a word, whereas sobriquet sounds more glamorous, more mysterious even. To refer to *The Eternal City* as a *nickname* for Rome will not quite answer, but *sobriquet* sounds well. Just as *The Big Apple* can be known as the nickname for New York without any disharmony. Famous *sobriquets* for people include the wonderful 'Teflon Man' coined by Pat Schroeder for Ronald Reagan.

Talisman

A talisman is an amulet, something worn to protect the wearer, or to bring good luck. It is often used in the religious sense, so that a small cross worn or carried by a Christian would be a talisman, as would any special ring, coin or artifact intended to bring 'good luck'. Although the idea of such ignorant superstition belongs to an irrational age, many of us still cling to the idea that touching wood has talismanic power.

Uxorious

Uxoriousness might be defined as what women think they most want, but only until they get it – the attentions of a foolishly fond husband. The problem lies in uxoriousness lying somewhere between the ideas of *devotion* and of *submission*, the one being desirable in a husband, the other not. Thinking about Wuthering Heights: Edgar Linton *is*, Heathcliff *isn't* – who do women appreciate most? Thus, uxorious men are not appreciated by anyone, hence it's almost universal use as a pejorative term. Mr Bayham Badger in Dickens' *Bleak House* is another good example of an uxorious husband from literature.

*V*enal

Some people may be bought, others may not. Venal is the word to describe those who may. The soldier turned mercenary, the government official who takes a bribe, the woman who marries for wealth alone – all are venal. It is a pejorative term which suggests that the venal person is prepared to waive his or her integrity for money. For those to whom this word brings to mind the contemporary corruption of the 'cash for honours' affair, it is worth remembering the biblical observation that 'the love of money is the root of all evil'. It is a most useful, succinct way to describe a human failing that people of discretion have *always* despised: 'there is nothing new under the sun', to use still more biblical wisdom!

$\mathcal{W}$idget

I often use this word as a synonym for *thingamajig*, when I can't remember the proper name for a thing. But what is the difference between a *widget* and a *gadget*? They are both small, sometimes mechanical, appliances made to perform a particular job, but for some reason I prefer 'widget' to 'gadget', possibly because it is a softer word, more pleasant to say and to hear. There is also an element of size and complexity perhaps: a stapler is a gadget, but a staple *remover* is a widget. A lever-style corkscrew is a gadget, but a foil-remover is a widget.

So widget can be used as a generic word for any designed thing that is a small and useful tool – especially one that doesn't really have a name of its own other than a long description – 'that thing for helping spiders to climb out of the bath', for example. Unfortunately, widget is also the word for a *symbolic* gadget, used in business wherever a hypothetical product is needed to illustrate a manufacturing or selling concept. Oh, and it's used in computing, but that's another story.

Xenophilia

This is the antonym of *xenophobia*, which is often used inexactly as a synonym for *racialism*. Xenophiles love foreigners and foreign cultures – manners, ways of life, foods, architecture and such – not just cheap alcohol, warm climates and beneficial exchange rates. On a more risqué note, xenophilia also describes sexual desire for complete strangers, as in the modern phenomenon of *dogging*. For many people this takes us straight back to *anomie* ....

$\mathcal{Y}$*omp*

I have included this word because although it is a neologism it has such a precise meaning and it sounds so wonderful. Yomping is Royal Marines slang for marching a long distance carrying full kit. The British Army uses *tab* rather than *yomp* – an acronym for Tactical Advance to Battle, but yomp is by far the more interesting word, taken from the acronym Your Own Marching Pace.

It has come to mean any longish hike over difficult terrain carrying a heavy load, although there is the implication of necessity or urgency about 'yomping' that is absent from 'hiking'. The most famous and admirable yomp was that undertaken by the armed forces after their landing at San Carlos during the Falklands War.

Zeitgeist

This is used quite widely and correctly to mean the intellectual and cultural climate of the age; at its simplest it may be used to mean the 'ethos of the time'. In the 19th Century, the German Romantics perceived the Zeitgeist to be more than just a concept – it was (as it were) the personification of the Spirit of any age.

Artists of all kinds try to distill the zeitgeist in their work. Because of this it is a useful term to know when discussing, for example, cinema – some films seem to grasp the essence of how the world is at a given period and zeitgeist is often used when reviewing bleak, uncomfortable films like *Trainspotting* and the classic *Bladerunner*. It would take a whole book, and I suspect a great deal of acrimony, to discuss the zeitgeist of this age as expressed in our popular music culture and in television's *Big Brother.*